WICCAN SPELLS

A Wiccan Book of Shadows!

Your Personal Spell Book!

Table of Contents

Introduction

I want to thank you and congratulate you for downloading the book, *"Wiccan Spells"*.

This book contains proven steps and strategies on how to understand the Wiccan book of shadows.

Before we start your Wiccan journey, you need to receive your first Wiccan greeting. Merry meet! No, it is not a spell right away since you will learn more about it in the second chapter. Merry meet happens to be one of the verbal greetings that most Wiccans exchange with their fellow Wiccans.

Have you ever wondered why Wicca is so attractive? Perhaps your friends, family or neighbors are Wiccans themselves. As early as now, Wicca is a religious belief that does not mandate laws to its coven or brethren. You are free to discover your calling since it is known to be a religion of preference. You can develop a religion or follow an existing religion that is relevant to your beliefs.

We are so thankful that you found this book that will teach you the proper way to cast a spell. You often wondered if spells are bad and they come back to you by seven-fold. For you see, not all spells are evil. That is why, in the first chapter, all the known Wiccan branches are provided so you can acquaint yourself with the Wiccan history.

In the next chapter, you will have the first glimpse of the Book of Shadows. Wiccan witches have this book in their possession. Since you are a dedicant or neophyte Wiccan, the Book of Shadows goes beyond your typical diary. What is written inside sets it apart from the others.

Once you make up your mind to go permanent with your out town responsibilities, the least you can do is to purchase popcorn. Good thing is that in the succeeding categories you will choose, it is best to evoke the gods and goddess to purify your empty, dirty water gallons.

Thanks again for downloading this book, I hope you enjoy it!

information herein, either directly or indirectly.

Respective authors own all copyrights not held by the publisher.

The information herein is offered for informational purposes solely, and is universal as so. The presentation of the information is without contract or any type of guarantee assurance.

The trademarks that are used are without any consent, and the publication of the trademark is without permission or backing by the trademark owner. All trademarks and brands within this book are for clarifying purposes only and are the owned by the owners themselves, not affiliated with this document.

Chapter 1. Understand Wiccan from its Past

Let this chapter make it clear that no part of the entire book has inclinations toward Devil-worship and most of all, hardcore Witchcraft. There will be no voodoo spells, incriminating chants and unexplainable offerings.

The Wiccan mission is overwhelming at first but once you embrace their beliefs, you will thank yourself in finding "The Absolute Truth". However, Wiccans do not claim that their religion is the one and only since they believe that all religions are valid to the person who believes in its validity.

This may be a relief to some but you have to know that Wicca does not believe in the Devil. Wicca does not welcome worshippers of Satan, nude offerings or other bestial actions. They, in fact, deny this principle, theory or belief since this religion is all about harmony and peace.

Are you familiar with nature worship? Venerating gods and goddesses? Then you can understand an eclectic religious belief called Wicca. It is actually based on the harmony of nature and spiritual beings. The objective of this religious belief is focused on love, reincarnation, prestige, karma and power.

Wiccan Branches

In order to fully understand what kind of Wiccan belief you will imbibe in your life, you need to know what its branches are. There are eight Wicca branches that were uniquely founded by its head priests or priestess.

1. **Alexandrian**

2. **Celtic/Gardnerian**

3. **Circle**

4. **Dianic**

5. **Faery**

6. **Frost**

7. **Gaia**

8. **Seax**

Alexandrian Wicca

- Founder: Alex Sanders (King of the Witches)

- Coven Established: 1960, United Kingdom

- Language: British

- Ceremonial Rituals: Magic elements

- Coven Gatherings: 8 Solar Sabbat Festivals, Full moons, and New moons

- Coven Mantra: Only a witch can convert a follower to become another witch

Celtic or Gardnerian Wicca

- Founder: Gerald B. Gardner (Father of Wicca)

- Coven Established: 1950, United Kingdom

- Language: British

- Ceremonial Rituals: Pagan-Esoteric, Judeo-Christian, Qabalah-Archangel system, Neo-druidism, and Magickal elements

- Coven Gatherings: Full moons, and New moons

- Coven Mantra: Mantra is revealed by invoking and staring at a Blue Star

Circle Wicca

- Founder: Kim Alan and Selena Fox (High Priestess)

- Coven Established: 1974, Madison, Wisconsin

- Language: English

- Ceremonial Rituals: Theurgy (the divine work), Thaumaturgy (the working of wonders), and Shamanism

- Coven Gatherings: Full moons, and New moons

- Coven Mantra: Help a lost soul return to its proper place (on earth or spirit world)

Dianic Wicca

- Founder: Zsuzsanna Budapest (High Priestess, Founding Mother)

- Coven Established: 1970, U.S.A.

- Language: English

- Ceremonial Rituals: Oak Groves worship (outdoor nature worshipping)

- Coven Gatherings: 8 Solar Sabbats, Full moons, and New moons

- Coven Mantra: The Goddess is the center of life.

Faery Wicca

- Founder: Tuatha De Danann

- Coven Established: undefined

- Language: Irish

- Ceremonial Rituals: Esoteric Christian, Druidism, Metaphysics, and Magickal enchantments

- Coven Gatherings: 8 Solar Sabbats,

Full moons, and New moons

Frost's Wicca

- Founder: Gavin Frost, Yvonne Frost (Priest and Priestess)

- Coven Established: 1968, West Virginia

- Language: English

- Ceremonial Rituals: Self-initiation, 8 Solar Sabbats, Magickal working

- Coven Gatherings: Full moons, and New moons

Gaia Wicca

- Founder: Kisma K. Stepanich

- Coven Established: 1985, USA

- Language: English

- Ceremonial Rituals: Magickal working, No Self-initiation, 8 Solar Sabbats

- Coven Gatherings: Predominantly female group meets over monthly esbats, full moons, and new moons

Seax Wicca

- Founder: Raymond Buckland (High Priest)

- Coven Established: 1974, USA

- Language: English

- Ceremonial Rituals: Self-initiation, Self-dedication and Solitary practice

- Coven Gatherings: Full moons and new moons

Chapter 2. How to Create Your Book of Shadows

For every Book of Shadows, its respective owners should follow an outline that has been passed on from generation to generation. It is also one way of identifying the contents of the BOS. Here is the suggested outline for your Book of Shadows. You may revise it accordingly but it will do you good if you check with your priest or priestess if you are doing it right.

- **Coven Laws**
- **Dedication**
- **Tables on Correspondence**

Coven Laws

Written on Page 1 of your BOS, the Coven Laws should include the acceptable behavior that each and every follower in your coven should follow. But what will happen should you become a Solitary Wiccan? Then the rules that you want to follow is written. Just like any coven, the Creed is written down in a notebook or book. It contains all there is to know about a particular brethren. If you want to create your own "diary of spells" you need to call it as your Book of Shadows (BOS). The BOS is a considered as one of the sacred tools in Wiccan religion. It also needs to be consecrated by your coven's Priest or Priestess.

For you see, with any coven, group or community, there is that one law that governs all. The Wiccan Religion has the Wiccan Rede. Written in the Rede is a key moral system that should be followed by everyone. They believe that you can do anything you want for as long as you harm no one. Did you know that the Wiccan Rede is a poem? The Witches' Creed was written by Lady Gwen Thompson in 1975.

Most historians, Wiccan followers and students believe that it resembles the 10 Commandments. Out of the 24 lines, there is one entry that summarizes the Wiccan lineage. "If it harms none, do what Thou Will!" The original creed is longer since it was written in archaic language. Nevertheless, an English translation was done to the joy of its American brethren.

To further justify the most important 8-words in the Wiccan Creed, Wiccans believe in the role of Karma in their life. It was mentioned in their books that once a person create 3 good deeds in a row, it may be rewarded with bad deeds in a row. This law is widely known as the 3-Fold Law.

Dedication

In the premise that you are already part of a coven, then you need to include a "dedication" as one of your Book of Shadow contents. What does it contain?

- Your initiation ceremony copy if part of a coven

- For solitary initiation, you need to discuss in a lengthy essay that you have chosen to observe, venerate and follow. You may always highlight this area by writing, I, (name), dedicate myself to (God or Goddess) today, (date).

The importance of dedication is self-introduction to a god or goddess in your coven. You declare that you would like to know these gods and show you the way to respect and love the 4 Elements. The desire to learn is important even if you are uncertain if you can go deep into finding out what your god or goddess plans you to do.

Part of the dedication is the Promise or Vow. This is often called as the Promise Mantra. Wherein you need to write down what you plan to do for your God or Goddess. Did you know that you can cite your vows in this section? As an example, you dedicate the Dedication ritual within the BOS as your Vow to Volunteer Work, Vow to Preserve Nature, and Vow to Recycle Materials.

Included in this ritual to complete the Book of Shadows, you need to offer food and drinks for two. You have to offer them to the God and his Goddess. Most brethren opt to offer juice, wine, cake or bread. After the offering, you call unto your God or Goddess. Having the food blessed, you need to eat what you offered so as not to waste the blessings.

Tables on Correspondence

Inclusion of the tools you will need to cast a spell is required in the Book of Shadows. You also need to write down their tasks, meanings and end results once the spell is cast. Also needed in this section are the different Phases of the Moon. Keep in mind that Wiccans are Moon-Phase dependent.

One of the famous Wiccan rituals concerning the phases of the moon is called Esbat. It is focused on the full moon so expect a lot of Wiccans to gather their coven to venerate the moon's full cycle. They cast spells by drawing a circle and evoke the Moon Goddess or Diana for protection, healing and prosperity.

Eight Solar Seasons of the Sabbats

Sabbats are 8 Wiccan holidays that are celebrated in a year. They are also follows:

1. **Samhain**

This holiday happens every year on

October 31. As dedicant Wiccans, the date is one of the most awaited holidays known as Hollow's Eve or Halloween. Samhain represents the cycle of life wherein one is brought to life while another passes away to next realm.

Wiccans believe that during Samhain, the veil that separates the spirit world from the living turns so thin that you can easily evoke a dead man's spirit.

2. **Winter Solstice (Yule)**

Yule is all about new beginnings and the Wiccan community is more than grateful to welcome this period. For you see, magickal workings are potent during this time since has an ample dose of warmth and light. Of course, Winter Solstice is Christmas Season so the atmosphere brings more people closer to the hearth of their homes.

3. **Imbolc**

This Sabbat reminds Wiccans that after the cold Solstice, spring is on its way. The Imbolc Sabbat comes every February so it is the start of your re-awakening. During the month, Brighid, the goddess of fertility and fire is evoked. It is the time to focus on planting crops if you are into farming.

4. **Spring Equinox (Ostara)**

Wiccans come to rejoice when the month of March arrives. They celebrate the Spring Equinox and give thanks to its coming since the crops are getting ready to bloom. If you plan to get pregnant during the Ostara, you may do so since it is the time for fertility.

5. **Beltane**

Happening every April, the Beltane is one of the Wiccan holidays that give thanks to the received abundance. The magickal elements are ready to be used, stars in aligned and the Goddess of fire and fertile womb or soil is evoked. The union of these factors give the Wiccans the chance to give thanks and celebrate that the first few months is not left barren by the gods.

6. **Summer Solstice (Litha)**

The crops, plants and flowers have bloomed by the month of June. Midsummer is one of the months that where Wiccans celebrate and give thanks for longer daylight hours. They did not hex the Winter Solstice but rather, embraced it and wished it over soon. Litha is celebrated through dances, eating and revelry.

7. **Lammas**

This holiday is one of the much-awaited Wiccan Sabbats. The reason behind the magic of Lammas is that harvest season is coming really soon! Everyone rejoices that their fertile lands where spared from sickness and other infestations.

8. **Autumn Equinox (Mabon)**

Every September 21, Wiccans converge to celebrate the Mabon to celebrate the closing of the Harvest season. This is the time when the fields are beginning to empty since the crops have been plucked away. This mid-harvest time needs prayers that another harvest season will bring luck and bounty.

Sacred Text

Your Book of Shadows must contain prayers, incantations or spells that you chance upon in different books or websites. Keep them footnoted so when you need more data about it, you can always go back. Did you know that you can make your own sacred text? All you have to do is write it down, recite a spell to bind it. These sacred texts will be included in your spells but keeping them arranged is the challenge. If you bought a 3-hole binder, good job on that since all you have to do is keep adding loose paper in a particular category.

To keep your Book of Shadows in one place, make tabs your new BFF. It will color code your spells, coven gatherings or even solitary invocations if you plan to do Wicca on your own.

Chapter 3. Invest on Tools Used in Wiccan Spells

As a true Wiccan, you would need the right tools in order to successfully undertake your spells. According to the Book of Shadows, these tools direct a certain amount of frequency to make the spell potent and lasting. For starters, acquaint yourself with the following tools described below.

Pentacle

Every Wiccan has this flat wood that has magical inscriptions carved on it. Most Wiccan neophytes often mistake the pentacle with the pentagram. You create a pentacle and turn it into a pentagram. The pentacle is a tool that represents the earth element or divine protection. As for the pentagram, it is a tool that has the 5 elements – air, water, spirit, earth, and fire. You use the pentacle to consecrate another tool or a circle.

Besom

Harry Potter broke his Nimbus 2000 so you need to look for a sturdier one. Yes, as a Wiccan witch, you need a broomstick to cleanse a particular area from negative energy. You use the besom before and after a ritual. In looking for the perfect besom, do search for those that have birch twigs, willow binding and ash staff. Should they become difficult to look for, any broomstick made from natural materials will do just as well. Keep in mind that as a Wiccan witch, broomsticks are not purchased for flying nor do astral projections.

Athame

Wiccans need tools that can direct the flow of energy towards it. Another tool as powerful as the besom is the Athame. These are double-edged knives that you may use for certain rituals. They are intended for cutting cords or chopping herbs needed for spells. You channel the energy to welcome the elemental guardians from the North, South, East, and West to join you. Bear in mind that these knives can be bought and not handed down from one Wiccan to another. Try not to haggle on the price to get it at a cheaper amount. You need to purchase it with a pure heart for it to work properly on your rituals. You pronounce Athame as a-tha-may.

Cauldron

By now, you are slowly welcoming in the fact that witches do exist in real life. They do not look scary as illustrated in movies but rather, beautiful or handsome as you are! Did you know that Wiccan witches know no gender? Men are no called warlocks, mind you. Anyway, what is the cauldron for? In most Wiccan covens, a brewing vessel is needed to cook the spell ingredients. This cauldron is a 3-legged cast-iron pot that you may purchase anywhere. The cauldron also symbolizes the water element and the female god.

Censer

The incense burner is one of the important tools to have for a Wiccan ritual. It is actually a cup or a bowl that you can use to burn incense and inhale the vapor afterwards. By using the Censer, you evoke the air element in the ritual; it is placed before the altar for your gods and goddesses.

Bell

Purchase a bell to ward off negative energy before you perform a ritual. Wiccan religion believes that the vibrations emitted by the bell become a great energy source when invoking the Goddess. It is also believed to provide harmony within a consecrated circle.

Chalice

You do not need a cauldron to mix small amounts of ingredients for your potion. What you need is a small goblet called a chalice that can hold salt water for cleansing. The chalice is an important vessel you can pour wine in for specific rituals.

Wand

Ceremonial Wiccan traditions make use of a phallic symbol that represents the male energy or fire element. You need to look for a wand to represent the male energy since water is usually of female energy. You will need a wand for consecrating a place or evoke a spirit. Keep in mind that Wiccan wands are not made of phoenix feather rather willow, oak or elder wood.

Candles

Every Wiccan gathering will not be complete without lighted candles. Apart from representing a god or goddess, candles are used to anoint new followers, consecrate a circle, and consecrate a Wiccan tool. Provided below are the candle's colors so you will know what you are lighting on.

- Gold – Money, understanding cosmic influences, fast luck.
- Yellow – Imagination, creativity, persuasion, and unity.
- Pink – Affection, honor, romance.
- Red – Strength, fertility, passion, courage.
- White – Cleansing, truth seeking, spiritual enlightenment and clairvoyance.
- Blue – Love, fertility, and wisdom.
- Black – Meditation, banish evil thoughts and channels in positivity.
- Silver – Positivity, psychic ability,

stability.

- Orange – Ambition, confidence, career.
- Purple – Idealism, secret ambitions, money, contact with spirit world.

Wiccan Tool Consecration and Purification

Consecrate and purify the tools that you will use to create a spell, potion or invocation. Begin by making a sweeping action with a besom. Go through the process of casting your circle.

1. Get four markers that will represent the four wind directions – north, south, east, and west.
2. Bring yourself to stand in the middle of the imagined circle.

3. Evoke the gods and goddess by reciting:

   "To strengthen my energy, I cast the circle I am in to shield me from harm. I bring forth and summon all positive and balanced energies to end this circle."

4. Remain in the center of the circle and recite as follows:

   "Watchtowers and guardians of North, south, east, and west; I call upon thee. Elements of my guardians protect me from the ill effects of air, water, fire and wealth."

5. Evoke gods and goddesses of the

elements; recite the following:

"I cast this circle in your presence my gods and goddesses. Bring my magic to disperse into the unknown realms of the Universe and end my circle."

6. Pass the Wiccan tools above the Censer; recite, "I consecrate and purify these tools to banish negative intentions to harm other people."

Chapter 4. Wiccan Gods and Goddess to Evoke

Wiccans believe that there is a god and a goddess that they can evoke, revere, and follow. In order to welcome their presence in one's life, they should undergo rituals, keep silent and perform rituals. Majority of coven members understand the deity (god and goddess) is a representation of their innermost dreams in life.

Through revering these deities, they need to personalize them so it will be easier to channel the energy for invocation. For the gods, here are some of the names and their personalities. Go through each of them and when you find the deity that is for you, your heart and soul with recognize it. One advice to a dedicant or neophyte Wiccan, when you need to know your god and goddess try not to choose a pair just because they bring abundance in wealth, fertility and wisdom. Actually, you should not choose them. They will choose you!

When will you find out that the deity already chose you?

- Presence of the deity via dreams or real-life vision.

- Animal, color or any representations of the deity is revealed in your everyday life.

Once the god or goddess choose you, they need to contact you several times. It does not happen in random. You will understand that there is a pattern that is not difficult to notice. Everything will be revealed to you at proper time and place.

However, there is a clear difference between evoking a deity from invoking one. For you see, when you evoke a being, you are calling it and asking it to be with you in a ritual. You have this intent that the being will eventually show up.

On the other hand, when you invoke a being or deity, you offer your body to be possessed by it. Since you are new to Wicca, it is advisable to hold off the act of invoking since you are not sure if you can withstand the possession. You are literally asking the being to take control of your body. This will be on a temporary basis or if you cannot win over it, it takes over your body permanently.

There are different kinds of deities you should know of. These are spirits that will be the focal point of your worship. There is The All, The Lord, and The Lady. What sets them apart is their purpose in your life.

The All

The spirit which governs The All is both god and goddess. In short, they are 2 halves of 1 whole. This means that The All is a lady and at the same time, a lord. In the Wiccan religion, you revere both manifestations. Ask any Wiccan and they will tell you that they admire The Lady for her compassion; the Lord for his focus.

Wiccan God or Lord

The Lord is there to help you regain your strength, and agility since he is the deity of protection. The Lord is like a father that will make sure you are cared for. He will show his presence when you feel weak and distraught. Evoke his support when you are feeling down and out. Yet, just like any father, he is known to show his wrath when you do not follow what he wants of you. That is why, when the wrath is released, his counterpart, the Lady, will soften the blow. The Lord takes different forms of deities and is often referred to as the following (to name a few):

- Apollo – Deity of Healing and Protection
- Babalu Aye (Yoruba) – Deity of Cures for Illnesses
- Cernunnos – Deity of Power and Masculinity

- Eros - Guardian of Love
- Frey - Guardian of Nature
- Lugh – Guardian or Deity of Skills
- Hephaestus – Guardian of Technology
- Thor - Guardian of Protection and Fertility
- Thoth - Guardian of Wisdom, magick, and writing
- Osiris – Guardian or deity of Resurrection and Fertility

Wiccan Goddess or Lady

Once you revere the Lady, you admire her personality that shows her nurturing side. She is present to shield you, help you grow and understands the journey of bringing a child on earth. The Lady encourages family connections. She takes different forms of deities that can be named as the following (to name a few):

- Abonde (winter goddess) – brings prosperity and fertility.
- Adraste – Guardian of destiny.
- Aphrodite –Deity of Beauty, and Love.
- Arianrhod – Guardian of life, and fertility.
- Cerridwen – Guardian of wisdom, magic, and wife to Hades (god of the Underworld).
- Danu – Guardian for abundance.
- Fortuna - Guardian of Chance and Destiny
- Maat - Guardian of Balance and Truth and Balance
- Sarasvati - Deity of Music,

Knowledge and Poetry

- Sophia – Deity of wisdom

Chapter 5. Wiccan Herb Concoctions

Wiccan witches have tried and tested different herbs to make their potions. These natural herbs are widely available in the market so it will not be difficult to procure them. As a neophyte or dedicant, acquaint yourself with some of the familiar herbs to know what they are for.

To enhance spells during a ritual, you need to sprinkle herbs on a lit candle. It is believed to add an extra surge of power to the spell. You may also place a little amount of these herbs in particular areas at home to remove bad energies.

Wiccans usually carry a small bag of herbs in their bags to shield them from danger especially when they go outside their homes. A common practice to evoke the power of herbs is to leave them under the moonlight on a full moon.

It will be a surprise to find out that there are some of the famous herbs you use in your kitchen. Know more about their charm and power below.

Alfalfa

Protection from bankruptcy, strengthens resistance to fight infection, aids digestion, and treats alopecia in women or baldness in men.

Allspice

Attracts luck, draws in money, treats respiratory infection, strengthens willpower, reduces muscle pain, treats depression, and stress.

Aloe

Prevents accidents at home, prevents loneliness, heals wounds, and relieves heartburn.

Anise

Prevents nightmares, and purifies bathing water.

Basil

Wards off negative vibes, and brings good luck.

Chamomile

Enhances sleep, attracts luck when used for gambling, clears head from worries, reduces stress, dispels curses, attracts love, protect from evil.

Hawthorne

This herb repels paranormal entities from your house. The entities are usually spirit wanderers or aptly known as ghosts. In the same time, fairies are attracted by the smell of this herb. They will help ward off bad spirits.

Lavender

Cast a love spell by using a bunch of these herbs. Aside from attracting a potential lover, lavender is known to induce a good night's sleep. Dreaming of your lover with this herb on your clothes or under the pillow will make him dream of you too.

Oregano

This herb brings in vitality, happiness, and strength.

Sage

This herb purifies, banishes bad vibes or negative energy.

Thyme

Attracts affection, banishes poor communication, and wards off negative thoughts among family members.

After getting acquainted with the power of these herbs, it is best to put them to work. As a dedicant Wiccan or a newbie, you need to write down these recipes in your Book of Shadows. Even though it is the age of technology already, using your own penmanship is better than just printing it on paper. Bear in mind that Wiccan spells come alive through the frequency of your unique vibration.

Before proceeding with the recipes, there

is one witch recipe conversion you need to understand. This is commonly seen in Wiccan potion recipes – 1 part, 2 parts, 3 parts and so on. To convert the measurements to layman's terms, you need only 1/3 tablespoon of a dried herb. Should you use fresh herbs, 1 part is equivalent to 1 tablespoon. With this conversion set to order, good luck on your potions!

Chapter 6. Spells, Recipes and Evocation Rituals

Aphrodite's Blended Tea

Enjoy this tea for existing or soon-to-be lovers. All you have to do is drink this aromatic tea for that unforgettable union.

Dried Ingredients:

- ➤ 1/3 tablespoons rose petals
- ➤ 1/3 tablespoons gingko leaves
- ➤ 1/3 tablespoons chips from cinnamon bark
- ➤ 1/3 tablespoons orange peel
- ➤ 1/3 tablespoons muira puama (Brazilian potency wood)
- ➤ 1/3 tablespoons peppermint leaves
- ➤ Stevia, to taste

Tools:

- ➤ Chalice

- Small cauldron
- Wand
- Censer
- Athame
- Pentacle
- Rose quartz or crystal
- Book of Shadows

Instructions:

1. Place all ingredients in a cloth bag and boil in a pot; steep cloth bag for ten minutes.
2. Once the water darkens, remove bag.
3. Pour tea in cups and add milk, Stevia or honey; drink while hot.
4. Keep a rose quartz nearby to successfully evoke the spirit of Goddess Aphrodite.
5. Write down the evocation to the

Goddess in your Book of Shadows.

"Oh Aphrodite, my Goddess of Beauty, and Love, I evoke you to fill me with your power. Help me in my purpose to be loved unconditionally by (state name of person). Help me oh Goddess to succeed through your help in this plea. I know you are the Goddess that showered me with your elegance and charm, turn my plea to help (state name of person) love me truthfully as I intend to him. Divert our minds from lustful tendencies as we begin the first step of our union that I asked for."

Venus' Tempest Brew

<u>Ingredients:</u>

- ➤ 1 oz. damiana leaves
- ➤ ¾ pint water
- ➤ 1 pint vodka
- ➤ 1 cup honey

<u>Tools:</u>

- ➤ Chalice
- ➤ Small cauldron
- ➤ Wand
- ➤ Censer
- ➤ Besom
- ➤ Athame
- ➤ Pentacle
- ➤ Book of Shadows

<u>Instructions:</u>

1. Begin the brew preparation by

making a sweeping action with a besom.

2. In a small cauldron, add vodka and damiana leaves; leave for 5 days to soak.

3. Strain the leaves in a coffee filter; add water and leave for 5 more days.

4. In the same cauldron, heat alcohol-infused water to 160°F and add honey.

5. Light the censer with a pink candle and inhale the smoke.

6. Store brew in a bottle and store for 30 days.

7. Strain extra sediments from the brew and serve in a chalice.

8. Lift the Athame to the chalice to direct the spirit of the goddess.

9. Lay down the pentacle near the

chalice for consecration.

10.   Drink the tempest brew every night and evoke the Venus, the goddess of love with an evocation passage from the Book of Shadows.

11. After the brew is finished, make a sweeping gesture to close the ritual.

12. Write down the evocation to the Goddess in your Book of Shadows.

"Oh Venus, my Goddess of Beauty, and Love, I evoke you to fill me with your power. Help me in my purpose to be loved unconditionally by (state name of person). Help me oh Goddess to be effective and successful in my plea."

Male Fertility Evocation Spell

<u>Ingredients:</u>

- ➢ 1/3 tablespoons Rice
- ➢ 1/3 tablespoons Rosemary
- ➢ 1/3 tablespoons Hazel Nuts

<u>Tools:</u>

- ➢ Wand
- ➢ Censer
- ➢ Besom
- ➢ Athame
- ➢ Pink Candle
- ➢ Pentacle
- ➢ Book of Shadows

<u>Instructions:</u>

1. Scatter rice on the floor.
2. Ward away misfortunes by a sweeping motion on the area where

the rice fell.

3. Light the censer with a pink candle, burn the rosemary leaves and inhale the smoke.

4. Lay down the pentacle near the Censer for consecration.

5. In a small bowl, place the hazel nuts and lift the Athame to direct the spirit of the god.

6. Eat the hazel nuts before evoking Cernunnos, god of male fertility.

7. Write down the evocation to the God in your Book of Shadows.

"Cernunnos! Cernunnos! Cernunnos! You are my Horned God. You tell me I am not separate from nature. My life strengthens and honors the connection to things that are living. You are my hunter god, Cernunnos. In order for me to live, something must die. My eating of these hazel nuts is the sacrifice of the Corylus tree that bore the source to feed me. I honor the ascendants before me who left a fertile hearth for my future descendants. Cernunnos, god of hunting and male fertility, I ask you to join me and bless me with your presence."

8. After the fertility spell is done, make a sweeping gesture to close the ritual.

Spell for Good Fortune

Tools:

> Besom

> Gold candle

> Holed-trinket (metal, brass, jade)

> Piece of string

> Pentacle

> Book of Shadows

Instructions:

1. Ward away misfortunes with a besom; make a sweeping motion around the area you are standing or sitting.

2. Light the gold candle, insert the string in the holed-trinket; knot the string once.

3. Situate the pentacle near the lighted candle.

4. Point the Athame at the candle to direct the spirit of the gods.
5. Pass the necklace above the lit candle.
6. Write down the spell in your Book of Shadows; recite the spell thrice.

"A candle is lit, as I pass the trinket over. Good fortune came my way. Energy, influence, wealth and knowledge come. My trinket, gain the power."

7. Wear the necklace and repeat the spell for as many times as you can.

Full Moon, Midnight Spell Incantation for Good Wealth

Tools:

> - 3 Gold candles
> - Besom
> - Athame
> - Pentacle
> - Book of Shadows

Instructions:

1. At the stroke of midnight, turn the light off the room and position the gold candles in one horizontal line; light them.

2. Situate the pentacle near the lighted gold candles.

3. Position the Athame next to the candles to direct the spirit of the gods.

4. Say three reasons why the deities you evoked should grant your wish of good wealth.
5. Utter what you intend to do in return of granting your wish.
6. Write down the spell in your Book of Shadows; recite the spell once.

"Oh powerful deities, grant me with a portion of your wealth. I come to you without any finances but now no more. I claim this wish be granted because (three reasons why). In return oh beloved, my revered deities, I will (what will you do when wish is granted). So mote it be! Diana, Goddess of the full moon, Lakshmi, God of Fortune and Odin, Norse Father God of Wealth, I evoke of thee to show me your powers."

7. Leave the candles to burn.
8. The following morning, leave the candles in place and anticipate their decision.

Weight Loss 3-Spell Incantation

<u>Tools:</u>

- ➤ Besom
- ➤ Athame
- ➤ Pentacle
- ➤ 1 Red Candle
- ➤ 1/3 tablespoons Water
- ➤ Book of Shadows
- ➤ 1 Apple

<u>Instructions:</u>

1. Cleanse your work area with a Besom to perform the opening ritual.

2. Take the red candle, light it and quietly meditate for 10 minutes; specify the number of pounds you

want to lose.

3. Situate the pentacle near the lighted red candle.

4. After meditating, get a medium-sized water container and submerge the apple.

5. Position the Athame next to the candles to direct the spirit of the gods.

6. Evoke on Venus, the goddess of Beauty,

7. Write down the spell in your Book of Shadows; recite three times.

   a. "Powerful Venus, Goddess of Beauty, I evoke on thee. Banish my weight gain. Make it happen as I submerge this apple in water. Heed my call Venus. Take my heaviness away. In return, I will provide healthy food to myself and my loved ones. Venus, Goddess of Beauty, I ask you to join me and bless me with your presence. Take my gluttony away and replace it healthy ways."

8. Eat the fruit and recite the invocation.

   a. "Take the fruit I eat and bless bestow upon me, the power to reject the junk that is making me weak. Help me, beloved Venus, to forget my glutton past. In return for your unconditional love, I will resort to exercises. Bring me closer to my goal and become a new body upon your grant."

9. Extinguish the flame from the red candle; recite the incantation to bind the spell.

    a. "Red candle, as I extinguish your flame, take my gluttony with you. Fill my new body with healthy food as I wake up to a new day. As I speak, so mote it be."

    b. Use the besom do a sweeping gesture to bind the spell.

Conclusion

Thank you again for downloading this book!

I hope this book was able to help you find your designated Wiccan god and goddess. It is with gratitude to receive several inputs from other fisher-folk. The Wiccan dedicant may find it difficult to comprehend at first. But it is surely a blessing that this book was purified by a real priest.

The next step is to get acquainted with different deities. They came from different parts of the country just to learn more about cauldrons, chalice, liquid receptacles, and use them in specific spells.

Finally, if you enjoyed this book, then I'd

like to ask you for a favor, would you be kind enough to leave a review for this book on Amazon? It'd be greatly appreciated!

Thank you and good luck!

Made in the USA
San Bernardino, CA
28 November 2018